ASIA
The
IMMORTALS

Illustrated by Chan Kok Sing
Translated by Koh Kok Kiang

ASIAPAC • SINGAPORE

Publisher
ASIAPAC BOOKS PTE LTD
629 Aljunied Road #04-06
Cititech Industrial Building
Singapore 389838
Tel: (65) 7453868
Fax: (65) 7453822
Email apacbks@singnet.com.sg

Visit us at our Internet home page
http://www.span.com.au/Asiapac.htm

First published May 1996

©1996 ASIAPAC BOOKS, SINGAPORE
ISBN 981-3029-98-6

Cover illustration by Chan Kok Sing
Cover design by Cheng Yew Chung
Body text in 8/9 pt Helvetica
Printed in Singapore by
Loi Printing

Publisher's Note

As a publisher dedicated to the promotion of works of Chinese philosophy, art and literature, we are pleased to bring you this graphic presentation of *The Eight Immortals*.

The Eight Immortals are among the most popular figures of Chinese myths and legends. In fact they are the legendary figures closest to the hearts of the ordinary people. The stories in this book show how eight ordinary people in ancient China attain immortality through selfless actions and good deeds. You will find out why Tieguai Li sells oil, how Zhang Guolao outwits the monks, and how Han Xiangzi tricks the emperor. You will also discover the relationship between Lü Dongbin and the Peony Fairy. The climax is, of course, how the Eight Immortals cross the Eastern Sea after attending the Peach of Immortality Gathering hosted by the Queen Mother. You will be enthralled by the vivid description of the great battle at the palace of the Dragon King.

We would like to take this opportunity to thank Chan Kok Sing for his lively comic illustrations. Our appreciation, too, to Koh Kok Kiang for translating this volume and writing the Introduction, and the production team for putting in their best effort in the publication of this book.

About the Illustrator

Chan Kok Sing is a Malaysian artist born in 1971. A lover of nature and the simple life, he enjoys physical exercise and reading. Upon completion of his secondary education in 1990, he took up a course in pure art at the College Of Art, Kuala Lumpur, and graduated in 1995. Since then, he has published many of his comics and illustrations in various newspapers in Malaysia. His aspiration is to have an art studio of his own.

About the Translator

Koh Kok Kiang is a journalist by vocation and a quietist by inclination. His interest in cultural topics and things of the mind started in his schooling years. It is his wish to discover the wisdom of the East that has kindled his interest in Eastern philosophy. He has also translated other titles in Asiapac Comic Series, namely *Book of Zen, Origins of Zen, Sayings of Lie Zi, Sayings of Lao Zi, Sayings of Lao Zi 2, Sayings of Zhuang Zi 2, Roots of Wisdom, Thirty-Six Stratagems, The I Ching,* and *Yue Fei.*

Introduction

Among the popular figures of Chinese myths and legends, the Eight Immortals of Taoist folk religion stand out.

They are probably the ones closest to the hearts of the ordinary Chinese as they represent all conditions of life—poverty, wealth, nobility, plebeianism, age, youth, masculinity and femininity.

Of the eight, three are said to be historical personages—Zhongli Quan, Zhang Guolao and Lü Dongbin. The others—Tieguai Li, Han Xiangzi, Cao Guojiu, Lan Caihe and He Xiangu—are mentioned in fables.

The Eight Immortals have been regarded by the Chinese with a special adoration because they signify happiness. As a result of this tradition, the number 'eight' has been favoured by the Chinese as representing luck or good fortune.

Like other human beings on earth, the Chinese regard happiness as one of the most important qualities in life. The stories about the lives of the Eight Immortals show that it is possible for ordinary mortals to attain immortality and lasting happiness through selfless actions and good deeds.

The legend of the Eight Immortals as a group is not older than the time of the Yuan dynasty (AD 1271-1368) although individual members had been previously celebrated as immortals in Taoist tales as early as the Tang dynasty (AD 618-907).

Most people see the Eight Immortals simply as the subject of charming stories though they actually play a more significant role. This is in relationship to the Bagua, or Eight Trigrams, of the Yijing (also known as the I Ching in English), the most popular classic of traditional China.

The Eight Trigrams are a series of three lines, which combine all possible variations of either a broken line or a full line. They form one of the most important sets of symbols in Chinese divination.

Each of the Eight Immortals is associated with a certain direction of the Eight Trigrams. In certain cases this is based upon their nature. He Xiangu, a woman, represents yin, the female principle. She is associated with the south-west and the three broken lines of the trigram which represents yin is placed there. Because of his hot temper, Tieguai Li is situated in the south while the calmer and the eldest of the Eight, Zhang Guolao, is in the north.

Zhang Guolao
張果老

Kan
坎

Cao Guojiu
曹國舅

Lan Caihe
藍采和

Qian
乾

Gen
艮

Zhongli Quan
鍾離權

Lü Dongbin
呂洞賓

Dui
兑

Zhen
震

Kun
坤

Xun
巽

He Xiangu
何仙姑

Li
离

Han Xiangzi
韓湘子

Tieguai Li
鐵拐李

Zhongli Quan, whose fan stirs the seas, is in the east where the sea meets China. Lü Dongbin, subjugator of the forces of evil and the unknown, is on the west, traditionally the dwelling place of the mysterious and magical due to the vastness of the deserts and mountain ranges which lie in that direction.

Han Xiangzi defends the south-east while the last two, Lan Caihe and Cao Guojiu, guard the north-west and north-east respectively.

The Eight Immortals and their directions along the Eight Trigrams are invoked in one of the most powerful forms of magic in folk Taoism. This is the Bazhen Tu, the Battle Chart of the Eight Trigrams, used to counter the work of practitioners of black magic.

Traditional China is said to embrace the San Jiao, or Three Religions, of Taoism, Confucianism and Buddhism. Most ordinary Chinese felt closest to folk Taoism as Confucianism appealed to the educated while Buddhism had been regarded as a foreign religion since its advent in China.

Literacy was a privilege of a few as the vast majority of the people were unlettered. Thus not many people were familiar with Confucian or Buddhist teachings. Folk Taoism had the greatest appeal to these people because its teachings were often in the form of fables which could be transmitted widely by story-tellers.

It comes as no surprise, therefore, that the Eight Immortals are manifested in the form of stories rather than philosophical works.

Stories about the Eight Immortals appeared at a time when Buddhism was making inroads into the Chinese world as great teachers were able to popularize it among the masses by simplifying Buddhist teachings. Followers of Taoism, China's native philosophy, wanted to maintain its place in Chinese thought and one means of doing so was to make it more accessible to the masses.

Stories about the Eight Immortals helped the Chinese to easily assimilate Taoist teachings and the tradition has continued to this day.

Koh Kok Kiang

Contents

Tieguai Li

鐵拐李

Tieguai Li is always depicted with his iron crutch and gourd which contains magic medicines. His original name was Li Xuan. His popularity seems to rest on his irascible and unpredictable character. Tieguai Li is the patron saint of druggists and exorcists.

Reincarnation After Repentance

Tieguai Li's original name is said to be Li Xuan
and he lived during the Sui Dynasty.

When he was
young, his
family was
very poor.
But he was
a very filial
son.

One year there was
a severe drought and
the harvest failed.

His father killed
himself in despair.

His mother wept so
much that she went
blind.

Tieguai Li felt
helpless.

He decided to go begging for food.

One day he noticed that someone had left a basket of carrots outside the house.

He decided to help himself to some of them.

Luckily for him his act went unnoticed.

Yippee! We are going to have carrots for dinner tonight.

My son, who is the kind soul who gave us so much to eat?

Soon it became a habit for him to steal.

3

It is so much easier to steal things than to beg for them.

Since then he had become habitually light-fingered.

Eventually he was caught red-handed.

People began to look at him with a jaundiced eye.

Every family would shut the door whenever he approached.

One night ...

He sneaked into someone's house.

4

If you are truly repentant, then return the wok at once.

Thank you for enlightening me!

That man saw that Tieguai Li was repentant.

Dawn was breaking …

Tieguai Li was worried that he would be apprehended when he returned the wok.

Please think of a way to help me.

Just go ahead and return it. When you have done so, come and see me. I intend to help you in some other way.

He raised his whisk and suddenly the sky turned dark again.

8

After those remarks, the man (a Taoist) disappeared.

The sky turned bright again.

Since then Tieguai Li had always been carrying the gourd with him everywhere to dispense medicine to cure sick people.

Eventually he went to live in a cave to practise the Tao.

One day, Laozi and Master Wan Qiu visited him and revealed to him the highest Taoist teachings.

9

On the sixth day …

Lang Ling, your mother is seriously ill.

He was a filial son and was anxious to see his mother. He cremated Tieguai Li's body.

Not long after, Tieguai Li was back.

He could not find his body.

While he was wondering what to do, he spotted the corpse of a person who had just died.

Tieguai Li decided to enter the man's body.

Why am I old and ugly?

12

Moreover, he was lame.

Oh, he is too ugly. I had better not use his body.

The action of Tao is not dependent on appearances. I'll give you an iron crutch to help you move about.

With this crutch, you can go anywhere.

Since then Tieguai Li roamed everywhere to help the sick and became one of the Eight Immortals.

Tieguai Li Sells Oil

A long time ago, the Eight Immortals Lake was originally a basin of land surrounded by mountains. There was a prosperous town situated in the basin.

But the townspeople did not acquire social graces despite their wealth and were crafty and wicked.

Are you putting this child as a stake?

The townspeople spent their time on wine and led a lustful life.

Indulgence in debauchery

Dragon King, unleash a flood of water to drown the townspeople!

There are good people among the bad ones. When the flood hits, the good people will be unjustifiably harmed as well.

All right, Tieguai Li, you go and look out for good people.

Tieguai Li and Han Xiangzi transformed themselves into beggars to visit the town. For three consecutive days, no one gave them food or money.

Eventually someone's baby defecated and the mother used one half of a pancake to wipe his bottom. She threw the dirtied half to the two beggars.

No, I maintain that we can find good people.

We can use this piece of pancake as evidence of the townspeople's wickedness to wipe them out.

The following day, Tieguai Li and Han Xiangzi transformed themselves into oil vendors.

16

Oil for sale. Ten coins for one gourdful, five coins for two gourdfuls.

Don't rush!

The oil jar was not big, but no matter how much oil was sold, the supply was not exhausted and they could not finish selling the oil as demand was great.

The townspeople thought that the oil vendors were fools and everyone bought two gourdfuls each time.

I'm giving you ten coins. Give me one gourdful of oil.

Eventually, a young girl approached.

Tieguai Li deliberately gave her two gourdfuls of oil for five coins.

Before long ...

I'm giving you 15 coins.

My grandfather said you counted wrongly. Now I'm here to make up the difference.

We have found good people at last. Ha! Ha!

I must inform my grandfather.

This place will soon be visited by disaster. When you see blood dripping from the eyes of the stone lion on Ten Characters Street, you must immediately flee to the mountains.

She told her grandfather about it and they went to look for the informants but they were nowhere to be found.

From that time onwards, the grandfather went to look at the stone lion every day.

He also told the townspeople about the matter.

The townspeople reacted with laughter and ridiculed him for talking nonsense.

Some of the townspeople decided to play a trick on him and daubed the eyes of the stone lion with pig's blood.

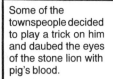

The following day, the old man came to take a look.

Everybody, take to the mountains quickly! Heaven is going to vent its wrath!

None of the townspeople believed him.

The old man and his granddaughter gathered their belongings and took their puppy with them up to the mountain.

20

Tieguai Li and Han Xiangzi reported their findings to the Jade Emperor.

Summon the Dragon King!

The Jade Emperor ordered the Dragon King to flood the town.

Dragon King, receive the edit ...

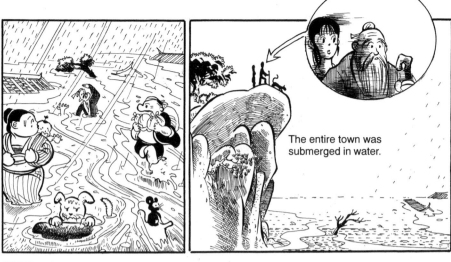

The entire town was submerged in water.

Grandfather, they are the ones who saved us.

Dear lass, how are you?

This is the consequence of wickedness.

Zhongli Quan
鐘離權

His family name was said to be Zhongli and he lived during the Han dynasty. Hence he is also known as Han Zhongli. He was said to have been a military officer. He is often shown bare-bellied and carrying a feathery fan which controls the seas.

Zhongli Quan Attains Immortality After Suffering Great Hardship

Zhongli Quan was from Yantai in Shandong Province and his father was a marquis. It was said that at the time of his birth a supernatural being entered the confinement room.

At the moment of his birth, the room was illuminated by a bright light which shone like raging fire.

Wah! Wah!

He was born with a round head and high forehead.

He did not cry, neither did he eat nor drink.

On the seventh day ...

I want to go to play in the Purple Palace and Jade Capital where the immortals live.

As a boy, he was fond of reading.

He also took up martial arts and swordplay.

He was of a chivalrous nature.

25

Help!

Hey!

Ouch!

These rascals deserve to be taught a lesson.

When he grew up, he became a general.

One day, he embarked on a military expedition to fight Tufan forces in what is now Tibet.

He was in charge of the troops.

As they were nearing the Tufan territory ...

Because of the superior size of the Tufan army and Zhongli Quan's lack of battlefield experience, the expedition ended in defeat.

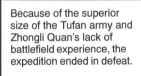

Zhongli Quan fled amidst the tumult.

He rode into a valley.

He then realized that he had lost his way.

Feeling exhausted, he was not inclined to find a way out immediately.

Suddenly a monk appeared in front of him.

Please follow me.

The monk led him to a manor.

Zhongli Quan dared not disturb the people
there and roamed about by himself.

Zhongli Quan was greatly surprised and knew that the old man was no ordinary person. Having just got out of danger, he was in no mood to leave and dropped to his knees.

He implored the old man to teach him the Tao.

Hmmm ...

The old man taught him the arts of immortality.

32

He learned about the Tao for a long time.

When he looked back after bidding the old man farewell, the manor had vanished into thin air.

Later, he met the Immortal Huayang and learned an even more profound way of Taoism.

From then on he wandered all over the country and finally realized the Tao on Si Hao Peak and became an immortal.

Bamboo Of Abundance And Ever-Full Mortar

Once, Lü Dongbin and Zhongli Quan were playing chess on Mount Tiantai.

Good! Moving my knight!

Ah Guang, a poor but honest and sincere man, was walking along the mountain path when he came across the two men.

34

He put down his shoulder pole to watch them playing chess.

It's hot. I'm going to eat a peach.

Lü Dongbin gave Zhongli Quan such a fright that he threw a peach backwards and it landed on Ah Guang.

Check!

No, it is because I was so eager to watch the chess game that I stood too close to you.

I'm sorry that it hit you.

Young fellow, if you don't mind my offer of a peach, you can eat it.

Ah Guang was feeling thirsty, so he took a bite.

It was a heavenly peach meant for immortals and after eating it, Ah Guang felt a surge of energy right through his body.

Don't throw away the other half of the peach. Take it home and you'll find that it will be useful.

Ah Guang was so engrossed in watching the chess game that he became oblivious of the passage of time.

Just before dusk, Ah Guang realized that he was still some distance from home.

Don't worry, just ride on my staff and before long you will reach home.

Ride this and I'll be home? Is it true?

Ah Guang rode on the bamboo staff and in an instant he was zipping through the clouds with the sound of the winds in his ears.

Wow! This is fast!

In just a moment, he arrived home.

As soon as he put the bamboo staff on the ground, it took root and began sprouting leaves.

Soon it turned into a gold bamboo grove.

Ah Guang shuddered and the other half of the peach that was tucked in his waist fell to the ground.

The peach turned into a gold mortar filled with money and jewels.

I like to be self-reliant and can't accept wealth that comes just like that.

If only the bamboo can turn green, then I can make utensils with it. If only the gold mortar can turn into stone, then I can use it to grind rice grains.

Just after Ah Guang had such thoughts, there appeared in front of him a grove of green bamboo and a stone mortar.

Ah Guang used the pestle to stir and grind the rice. The more he stirred the more rice he got.

Ah Guang distributed the rice to the villagers. As soon as he finished scooping up the rice in the mortar, it would be full again. Everyone called it the "ever-full mortar".

One day …

Uncle!

Oh, it's you, Ah Chong. Long time no see.

Uncle, you're great. Tell me where you got your ever-full mortar from.

Being a straightforward person, Ah Guang gave a full account of what had happened to him to his nephew who was nicknamed 'Lazybones'.

Next morning, Lazybones told his uncle that he wanted to take over his job.

Oh, this is tiring. How much farther must I walk!

As expected, Lazybones came upon Lü Dongbin and Zhongli Quan.

One is fat while the other is slim. They must be the immortals uncle talked about.

Come, let me give you a peach.

Check!

Lazybones ate the peach immediately and held on to the seed tightly.

Oh no, my stomach is rumbling. I would like to go home to clear my bowels.

Don't worry. Ride on this bamboo staff and you'll reach home quickly.

Is it true?

Lazybones was afraid that the gold bamboo might fly away and he tried to pull it up and hide it in his house. But his efforts were in vain no matter how hard he tried.

What's going on?

He fell down Golden Bamboo Ridge.

Help!

Since then a bamboo grove and a stone mortar had been seen at Golden Bamboo Ridge.

43

Zhang Guolao
張果老

He is said to have lived in the 7th or 8th century AD and is often pictured riding his donkey backwards. His symbol is the fish drum which consists of a bamboo tube with smaller tubes emerging at the top. He is venerated as one who brings male offspring.

He Shouwu And Guolao Temple

Zhang Guolao was born in a poor family and he made his living carrying goods on his donkey.

One afternoon, he led his donkey to a dilapidated temple hoping to get some rest.

Zhang Guolao had only a little food with him.

Shall I keep this piece for my dinner?

Just as he was leaving ...

Wow! Wonderful smell!

A delicious aroma wafted from the temple.

He decided to trace the source of the aroma.

He peered through the doorway of the temple.

There was no one in the temple but there was a wok with something being cooked in it.

The aroma came from the stew of a meat-like herb being cooked in the wok.

Strange! How come the cook did not eat the food at home but left it here at the temple?

The aroma is irresistible!

Zhang Guolao went out to take a look but did not see anybody.

He decided to use twigs to improvise as chopsticks.

He thoroughly relished the food.

Actually, there was a story behind the wok of food.

Not far from the temple was an eccentric teacher.

He sought immortality through physical practices.

Teacher, in that desolate spot is a bare-bottomed child who wanted to play with me.

One day, a student told him ...

It must be the shouwu herb spirit.

Whoever eats it will become an immortal.

Hence he thought of a way of tracing the source of the herb using a red thread and a needle.

He took hold of one end of the thread and asked his student to attach the needle holding the other end to the bare-bottomed child.

The following day, the boy appeared again to play and the student acted as he was told.

He followed the thread to find out where the shouwu spirit dwelled.

At the back of the temple, he spotted the shouwu plant.

He started digging.

It turned out to be a shouwu of good size.

He cooked the herb in the temple only to realize that he lacked eating utensils.

Just as he was on his way home to get eating utensils, he ran into an old friend.

Teacher, how about writing a pair of couplets for me?

After he had finished writing the couplets, his friend invited him to tea.

Meanwhile, back at the temple ...

Zhang Guolao could not finish all the food and noticed that his donkey appeared hungry.

He gave the remainder to the donkey.

He splashed what was left of the soup on a wall.

As he was leading his donkey away, he saw the highly agitated teacher approaching.

Oh no! The owner is here!

Time to flee!

Zhang Guolao and the donkey rose into the air.

The abandoned chopsticks grew into a pair of huge trees and became known as Guolao trees.

The wall of the temple on which the stew was splashed became as solid as iron and could not be toppled.

After the story of how Zhang Guolao became an immortal circulated among the people, the temple came to be known as Guolao Temple.

55

Zhang Guolao Outwits The Monks

Once Zhang Guolao went roaming in the mountains with his donkey.

He had been travelling for the whole day and was a little hungry. From the distance was the sound of a temple summoning monks to dinner.

Tang!

Tang!

Tang!

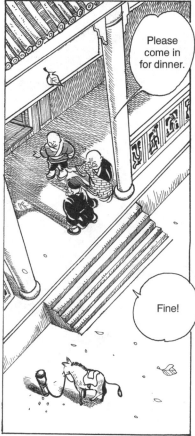

This food is delicious.

Immediately after eating, he walked out.

Zhang Guolao deliberately wanted to test the monks. After eating, he did not utter a word of thanks.

How brazen of him!

He appeared whenever it was time for meals.

Hey! Here I am again.

He always ate a lot of food.

As time went by, the younger monks began to resent his presence.

Even Buddhists have a temper!

The monks decided not to sound the bell for dinner but to strike the wooden fish instead.

Meal time!

But Zhang Guolao still showed up as usual for meals and left after eating.

How come the bell is not sounded today?

Oh, you're here again.

Finally, the young monks hatched a devilish plot.

One day, Zhang Guolao came to visit the temple and after his meal talked with the abbot about scriptures.

The young monks went to the back of the temple and killed his donkey.

They also dismantled the small bridge which Zhang Guolao used to cross over to the temple.

Ah!

Hee! Hee!

Zhang Guolao discovered that his donkey had been slaughtered.

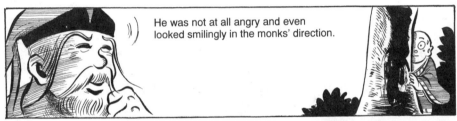

He was not at all angry and even looked smilingly in the monks' direction.

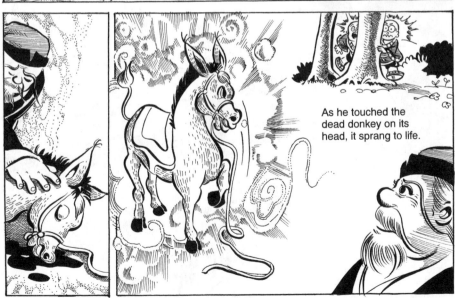

As he touched the dead donkey on its head, it sprang to life.

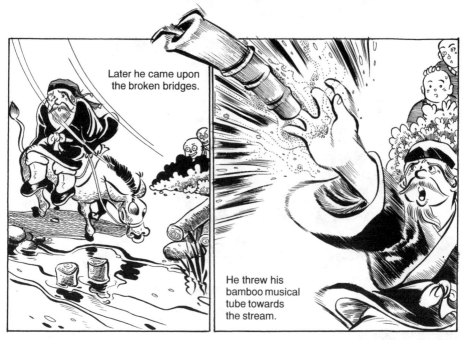

Later he came upon the broken bridges.

He threw his bamboo musical tube towards the stream.

Repentance is wisdom.

Immortal, we have wronged you. Please forgive us.

The bamboo musical tube turned into a bridge and Zhang Guolao rode his donkey across.

He drew a picture of a donkey.

In fact, Zhang Guolao had already regarded his donkey as dead and scattered pieces of its skin on the ground. Immediately a kind of seedling called "donkey meat" began to sprout.

Since then Zhang Guolao could always travel whenever he wanted by turning the paper donkey into a real animal.

Lü Dongbin
呂洞賓

Lü Dongbin is the most popular of the Eight Immortals. He is seen as a healer of the poor and a slayer of evil spirits. His symbols are a Devil Slayer sword and a bushy fly whisk which enables him to fly at will. Lü Dongbin is the patron saint of barbers.

Lü Dongbin Attains Immortality Through Perseverance

Lü Dongbin was born in the Tang Dynasty. His father and grandfather were court officials. When his mother was pregnant, an exotic fragrance filled the room and there was heavenly music.

A white crane descended from the sky.

Shortly, Lü Dongbin was born.

It flew into the room and vanished into his mother's womb.

Lü Dongbin had been exceptionally clever since young.

He could easily memorise and recite the Confucian classics.

When he was at Mount Lushan, he met the Fire Dragon Immortal who taught him advanced swordplay.

He went to Chang'an, the capital, twice to sit for the imperial examinations.

However, he was unsuccessful both times. He was then 42 years old.

One day, he was having a drink at an inn.

Zhongli Quan come.

Yes, please.

May I sit here?

You look downcast. Is something bothering you?

It was not easy for Lü Dongbin to find a person who understood him, so he told Zhongli Quan about all the things that turned out against his wishes.

They drank and chatted and before long Lü Dongbin fell into a drunken stupor.

Zhongli Quan took Lü Dongbin to rest at his hut.

As Lü Dongbin was resting, Zhongli Quan went to cook millet.

Lü Dongbin dreamt that he became the top scholar and rose steadily in his official career. He also enjoyed a blissful family life.

Eventually he became the prime minister and held the post for many years.

One day, he offended the new emperor who feared his influence and his entire family was executed. He was sent into exile and was in desperate straits.

Lü Dongbin awoke with a start and was gripped by fear.

You have finished your dream before the millet is cooked.

The greatest happiness in life is to be associated with the spirit, and the greatest misery is to know too much and yet be unable to be detached.

How do you know I was dreaming?

You must be an immortal. Please accept me as your disciple.

Sure, but there are conditions.

Zhongli Quan wanted to test his resolve.

One day, Lü Dongbin's entire family died. He felt no sadness. All he did was to make the funeral arrangements.

Having passed this test, his family rose from the dead.

Another day, after he had agreed on a price with a merchant, the man went back on his word.

He did not argue and paid the price.

On another occasion, he met a beggar and gave him some valuables. Not only was the beggar ungrateful, he also berated Lü Dongbin, who apologized for offending him.

He came across a tiger about to attack a flock of sheep and shielded them with his body.

At the sight of the imposing figure, the tiger turned around and fled.

Once while he was tilling the field ...

He found some gold coins.

He didn't even touch a single one and covered them up.

He bought a bronze vessel and when he reached home and realized that it was actually made of gold, he returned it to the seller.

Whoever eats it is sure to die, but he will be able to learn the Tao in his next life.

A Taoist was selling "sure-to-die" pills and no one dared to buy them.

However, no harm befell him.

It was the onset of spring and Lü Dongbin was crossing the swollen stream with others.

Suddenly the current became very strong.

All the people were crossing warily.

Ah!

Others became frightened but Lü Dongbin did not harbour any thoughts of life and death.

He remained composed.

Lü Dongbin went to live alone in a mountain hut.

One day a beautiful girl appeared.

She begged to go to bed with him.

Lü Dongbin felt no desire.

Once while he was alone at home ...

Many evil spirits appeared and wanted to attack him. He was completely unafraid.

Another night there appeared a ghastly figure who claimed that he was killed by Lü Dongbin in a previous life and wanted the blood debt to be repaid.

A killer deserves to be killed. This is logical and just.

Stop!

Suddenly there was a shout and all the apparitions disappeared.

Zhongli Quan appeared.

Lü Dongbin, you have passed my tests.

Zhongli Quan taught him to ride the clouds. Lü Dongbin practised Taoism for a long time and eventually became an immortal.

Lü Dongbin And The Peony Fairy

One day, Lü Dongbin was travelling in the vicinity of Mount Tongbai.

He saw that some houses were destroyed and the occupants had been killed.

Roar!

A giant pangolin was terrorising the people.

So it is that pangolin that is terrorising people. You need the jade hairpin of the Queen Mother to subdue it.

How can I get the hairpin?

There is a way. The Peony Fairy often goes to meet the Queen Mother. She has worldly thoughts. If you can win her affection ...

As he was talking, the Peony Fairy came to offer wine.

Just then ...

Lü Dongbin stealthily pinched her hand.

The Peony Fairy blushed.

What am I to do? This is against heavenly rules.

I had already seen through you.

Lü Dongbin conjured an earthly scenario.

See how loving couples are on earth!

The mortal world is full of delightful sights and sounds. Don't you like it?

She was still transfixed on the sight of the loving couple.

The humanly world is wonderful.

Lü Dongbin then told her what he had wanted her to do.

He showed her what was happening on Mount Tongbai.

The Peony Fairy eventually agreed on condition that Lü Dongbin and her lived as a couple for a hundred days in the mortal world.

Lü Dongbin asked her to exchange a fake hairpin for the real one.

The Peony Fairy accomplished the task.

The pangolin appeared again.

Watch out!

At Mount Tongbai ...

82

Charge!

Lü Dongbin flashed the jade hairpin.

The pangolin froze.

He had eliminated a source of evil.

Lü Dongbin descended after slaying it.

Lü Dongbin and the Peony Fairy lived as husband and wife for a hundred days in the mortal world.

Later, he left her ...

Cao Guojiu
曹國舅

According to one legend, he was the
brother of Empress Cao, mother of
Emperor Ying Zong of the Song dynasty.
He is shown wearing official robes and a
court head-dress. In his hands are an
imperial tablet and a pair of castanets.

Cao Guojiu Becomes An Immortal By Reformation

Cao Guojiu's original name was Cao Yi. Cao Yi was the emperor's uncle and thus came to be known as Guojiu (emperor's uncle).

Cao Guojiu and his two brothers were bullies.

They liked to hunt for pleasure.

After hunting, they would have a feast.

Your Lordship, we are going to have a windfall again.

A jewellery merchant and his wife were passing by the place.

Hey, merchants, why not take a rest and join me for a drink before you proceed.

They took up his suggestion and joined him for a drink.

I don't feel well.

Quick! Finish them off and seize the valuables.

Cao Guojiu had added a drug to the drink to knock them out.

Oh!

Suddenly a whirlwind descended.

When the wind died down, the drugged victims and the valuables were nowhere to be seen.

What's going on?

There must be spirits around!

That night.

Cao Guojiu had a frightful dream.

Cao Guojiu, pay with your life!

Hold it!

When the Taoist man appeared, all the ghosts disappeared. The Taoist man told him: "Repent before it is too late."

From then onwards, Cao Guojiu decided to make up for his past wrongdoings.

Whenever there was a famine, he would provide free food.

He also provided medical help by opening an apothecary. The poor did not have to pay for treatment.

Doctor, what's wrong with him?

He has a fever. These pills will cure him.

Cao Guojiu's two brothers strongly opposed what he was doing.

Our fortune will soon be gone.

He also set up a charitable home to house those who were unable to fend for themselves.

One morning ...

Your Lordship, this is terrible!

All the residents in the charitable home had been poisoned and Cao Guojiu was very sad over their deaths.

He was quick in getting to the bottom of the matter. His two brothers were responsible and he had them arrested and sent for execution.

Cao Guojiu travelled to learn the Tao. When Lü Dongbin saw that he had repented and was sincere, he helped him become an immortal.

Cao Guojiu Gets The Better Of The Textile Merchant

Once Cao Guojiu went to Bianliang, the capital of the Song Dynasty, from Hebei Province. He arrived at a jetty on the Yellow River. Two others were taking the same boat with him.

One was a craftsman and the other was a textile merchant.

Boatman.

They got on the boat.

The textile merchant had three cases of goods with him.

The craftsman had only one case of belongings while Cao Guojiu was empty-handed.

All of you must pay thirty coins each.

When the boat came to the middle reaches of the Yellow River, Cao Guojiu blew at the northwestern part of the sky.

In a flash a thunderstorm broke out.

This is dreadful.

The boat was tossing violently in the river.

Strange, how come there is a storm out of the blue?

Oh no, the boat is about to sink!

97

Quick, throw the goods into the river! Otherwise all of us will be in danger.

The craftsman was the first to throw his things into the river.

But the merchant steadfastly refused to throw away his goods.

The boatman did his best but the vessel still rocked violently.

If you still don't co-operate, I will jump into the river and leave you behind.

The merchant still could not bear to part with his goods.

I am going to save myself by jumping into the river.

The merchant had no choice but to follow the boatman's advice to throw away his goods.

Once the boat became lighter, the wind and rain stopped.

Inexplicable!

However, the men were unable to go ashore as the boat was some distance from the bank.

Boatman, lend me one of your oars.

Cao Guojiu hurled the bamboo towards the bank.

The oar was transformed into a walkway and the four men could safely go ashore.

Wait for me! Wait for me!

The boatman and the craftsman expressed their gratitude to Cao Guojiu for saving their lives.

Look, your belongings are floating here.

The craftsman was delighted to get his things back.

It dawned on the craftsman that Cao Guojiu was an immortal and he knelt to thank him.

Immortal, please get back my things for me.

Let me give you a piece of advice.

It does not pay to be miserly. Small advantages will cost you heavy losses!

The merchant felt humiliated.

If you will get my things back for me, I will be very grateful.

If he will turn over a new leaf, then his past will not be taken against him.

Han Xiangzi
韓湘子

He is said to be a nephew of the famous
Tang dynasty scholar Han Yu. His emblem is
the flute. A lover of solitude, he represents
the ideal of a contented person dwelling in
natural places. He did not know the value of
money and, if given any, used to scatter it on
the ground. Han Xiangzi is the patron saint
of musicians.

The Exquisite Sound Of Flute Moves Heaven

Han Xiangzi's parents died when he was young and so
he went to live with his uncle.

At the age of eight he could compose poetry and at the age of sixteen
he had passed the second highest level of the imperial examinations.

Some time later, Han Yu offended the emperor and was exiled.

He was exiled to Chaozhou, a poor and desolate place.

Overnight, Han Yu's residence became deserted and relatives and friends shunned the house.

Human emotions are fickle. What does high and low mean anyway?

Seeing how uncertain things were in mundane life, Han Xiangzi often went to natural surroundings and sought to know himself.

Han Xiangzi gave up reading Confucian literature such as the Four Books and Five Classics.

He spent his time playing a bamboo flute.

He also spent his time drinking tea or wine with talented people.

One day, Han Xiangzi went to the Lijiang River and saw an old man playing a flute.

The sound of the flute was refined and exquisite.

Marvellous! It's a wonder to hear something like this in the human world.

In a moment of exuberance, Han Xiangzi also played a tune with his flute.

Master Han, do you want to compete with me? Let's see who can attract the divine flute.

Based on what you said, I would like to give it a try.

Han Xiangzi began playing tunes he was familiar with on his flute.

This won't do. What you are playing are the same old tunes. How can it move the divine flute?

What should I do then?

You should travel to look for a really good teacher first.

Han Xiangzi left his uncle's mansion and travelled from place to place.

Somebody was playing a tune on a flute.

What a marvellous sound!

He went to trace the source of the music.

He saw a girl who was so absorbed in playing the flute that she did not notice him.

So she's the musician.

Lin Ying, you resemble my childhood playmate.

Her name was Xiaomei. Twenty years have passed.

I wonder how she is now.

Lin Ying, when I am with you, I have indescribable sweet feeling. I ...

Han Xiangzi had spoken what was in his heart.

I'm very sorry that I cannot accept your love. You see, I already have a partner.

No more was said that night.

Dawn broke.

Indeed Lin Ying had a fiance who seemed to have returned from a trip.

Han Xiangzi, that's the end of the matter.

Han Xiangzi wrote a poem to describe his feelings.

Han Xiangzi went to the Lijiang River and played the flute to express his sorrow.

This tune is very touching. I've never heard anything so moving.

The divine flute is appearing!

From the water appeared a lustrous jade flute.

You are now freed of worldly cares.

He practised the Tao and made progress.

Before long, with the help of the flute, Han Xiangzi attained immortality.

Han Xiangzi Tricks
The Emperor

Once there was an emperor who cared for nothing except self-indulgence and pleasure-seeking.

He oppressed the people and took away their valuables.

Han Xiangzi learnt that officials were making their way to the palace to offer gifts to the emperor on his birthday.

Good, here's my chance to teach him a lesson.

In a moment, Han Xiangzi had arrived at the Hundred Blossoms Palace in Luoyang.

Wow! What a lovely fragrance! What beautiful flowers!

Who allowed you to come here?

In a flash, Han Xiangzi was back in Chang'an.

He walked towards the palace gate.

I came to beg for alms.

Hey, w are y here f

Are you blind? Is this the place to beg for alms? Get lost!

Sure, I'll leave.

Han Xiangzi rose above the gate and towards the palace

Ha! Ha!

Supernatural being!

119

120

However hard they tried, they could not move the gold mountain.

Suddenly a fierce tiger leapt out of the gold mountain.

The fox changed back into a fairy which flew into Han Xiangzi's basket. The emperor was livid with rage.

Han Xiangzi guffawed and flew out of the palace.

Lan Caihe
藍采和

Lan Caihe is the strangest of the eight, being at times male and at times female. He is often shown carrying a basket of flowers. He represents the odd figure who does not fit into social categories. Lan Caihe is the patron saint of florists.

Lan Caihe Jumps On The Divine Raft

Lan Caihe was originally a barefoot deity in heaven. However, he offended the Celestial Lord and was banished to earth.

It's a male child.

Waa!

Lan Caihe was born in the family of official Lan who was delighted to have a male child at his advanced age.

When he was one year old, Lan Caihe became fond of books and lost interest in toys.

When he was three, his mother died of a serious illness.

His father remarried and had two more sons.

At a young age Lan Caihe could recite poetry and he was fascinated by *Dao De Jing*.

When he was eight, his father died.

Father!

His stepmother began to show her fierce nature.

She did not give him enough food or clothing.

127

Eventually she drove him out of the house.

In the day time he recited stories and poems to make a living.

At night he slept in a rundown temple.

Lan Caihe was hardworking and good-natured. The people were willing to help him.

129

130

The bamboo leaf grew in size and lifted Lan Caihe into the sky.

Although Lan Caihe was young, he became one of the Eight Immortals.

Lan Caihe And The Jade Board Bridge

One winter, Lan Caihe came to the Jade Stream at Nanyue. Suddenly there was a snowstorm.

It grew dark and Lan Caihe decided to pass the night outside an inn.

The innkeeper's son drank the wine with him.

Bottoms up!

You have a good capacity for wine. Bottoms up!

My father is Zhu Xiang. He calls me Zhu Zi.

My name is Lan Caihe. What's yours?

After drinking the wine, Lan Caihe did not say anything and left.

Zhu Zi followed him, only to find that Lan Caihe was clapping his jade board and singing in the street.

Lan Caihe's performance was very much appreciated by the audience.

Thank you! Thank you!

It grew dark.

Good!

Zhu Zi, let's go home.

On the way home ...

He saw that Zhu Zi had joined a group of children in playing hide and seek.

Zhu Zi behaved just like a child and his child-like nature was remarkable.

Children, come home. Stop playing.

If you play with him, you will become an idiot like him.

It turned out that Zhu Zi was slow-witted by nature. The villagers did not like to mix with him for fear that they would be affected.

That night, Lan Caihe went to the inn.

Mr Zhu, here's my payment for the wine.

There's no need to pay me. Please use the money to buy warm clothing for the winter.

Lan Caihe did not stand on ceremony and stayed on with the Zhu family. After six months, the three became close friends.

One day the Inspector-General of Hunan Province received an edict saying that the emperor was coming to Nanyue for a visit.

To ensure that the emperor had a pleasant trip, the Inspector-General decided to personally check the roads leading to Nanyue.

The bridge above the Jade Stream is too narrow.

I give you one month to build a bridge large enough for a carriage to pass through.

Fellows, hurry up!

As the time was short, the magistrate ordered the work to be speeded up.

Build another pier!

To his surprise, the pier of the bridge that was built during the day had disappeared at night.

Another pier was built but the same thing happened again. No matter what the magistrate tried, the pier could not be built.

The magistrate had no choice but to offer a reward to whoever could accomplish the task.

The person who can build the bridge over the Jade Stream will receive 200 taels of gold.

One day someone rose to the challenge.

It turned out to be Zhu Zi. The villagers were perplexed.

The following day, a military official came to summon Zhu Zi to build the bridge.

I did not take the notice.

But the officer insisted that he personally saw Zhu Zi taking it.

That night, Lan Caihe was back.

It was I who disguised as you to accept the task.

Building this bridge is no small matter. Failure can result in execution!

Zhu Zi, boldly go forward to build it.

Lan Caihe splashed a cup of wine on the wall. A drawing of the bridge appeared.

The piers were swallowed by a giant beast living in the Jade Stream. Tonight I will help you to eliminate it.

Lan Caihe went to the Jade Stream and burnt paper charms on a piece of rock there.

He then hurled the red-hot stone into the stream.

Indeed there was a giant beast which swallowed the stone in one gulp.

Ah, What is this?

The beast was burned by the red-hot stone. It changed into its original form which was a giant catfish.

Lan Caihe is giving this worm to you.

Only now did Zhu Zi perceive that Lan Caihe was an immortal. He built the piers according to Lan Caihe's drawing.

After finishing the task, Zhu Zi wondered where to get stones large enough to lay on the bridge.

Lan Caihe secretly helped Zhu Zi.

He took out one of his jade boards.

The jade board grew to a size large enough to cover the bridge.

Grow bigger!

Wow! What a lovely bridge!

Henceforth the villagers changed their feelings towards Zhu Zi. The bridge came to be known to later generations as the Jade Board Bridge.

He Xiangu
何仙姑

The only woman in the group, she is often shown holding a lotus bloom, the flower of open-heartedness, which reflects her nature. She is portrayed as an exceptionally beautiful maiden.

The Lotus Flower And He Xiangu

He Xiangu was a native of Niujiao county by the Huai River.

Her parents died when she was young and she went to work for an old woman when she grew up.

The old woman was lazy and made He Xiangu do all the chores.

146

He Xiangu had to work non-stop from dawn to midnight every day.

He Xiangu was kind-hearted by nature and would give food to the poor.

The old woman often beat her.

One day ...

I'm going out. You must grind the beans.

He Xiangu worked all alone. She poured the liquid made from the beans into a big wok.

At this time, seven people came to the door.

Have pity on us!

We have not eaten for three days.

Who are you all?

They had a gaunt look and wore ragged clothes.

Please!

Miss, help us!

He Xiangu was moved by their distress. She quickly gave a ladleful of soya milk to Tieguai Li.

The six others surged forward and He Xiangu was put in a difficult position as she knew that if the old woman returned, she would be punished for giving food away.

Please help us!

Am I not a poor person like them? I ought to help them.

You are all also poor people. I will give you soya milk even if I get beaten for doing so.

In no time they finished drinking the soya milk.

After giving their thanks to her, the seven men left.

Soon the old woman returned.

Soon she came upon them.

She told them what happened after they had left the house.

That's too much! We will go back with you.

The old woman was standing at the door.

All of you, return the soya milk to me.

Urgh!

All the seven men vomited the soya milk into the wok.

Having vomited, they left.

You wretch, drink up the soya milk they vomited.

154

I won't drink it!
The old woman took out her hairpin and heated it until it became red hot. She threatened to stick it into He Xiangu's body.

All right, I'll drink it.
Drink it all up!
After drinking it, He Xiangu felt like killing herself. She decided to get out ...
I don't want to die in this ghastly place.
Don't run!

The solitary lotus flower in the pond turned into numerous plants which covered the pond.

In the nick of time ...

He Xiangu rose into the air like an immortal.

The old woman could not catch up with her.

He Xiangu, thank you for the soya milk.

So you are the immortals!

Just now you drank the soya milk we vomited. It can neutralize poisons and make you an immortal.

He Xiangu became an immortal because of her kind nature. She is also the only female among the Eight Immortals. She has a refined and gentle look and is often seen holding a lotus bloom which she uses to cure the sick.

He Xiangu And The Horse-Landing Bridge

In Tiantai city in Zhejiang Province, there is a bridge shaped like a crescent moon. It is the famous Horse Landing Bridge.

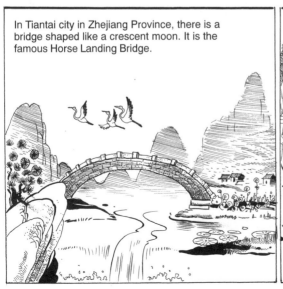

Legend has it that in a certain village there lived an industrious and honest herbalist.

All year round, he roamed everywhere to look for herbs.

He often had to climb steep crags to collect herbs.

One day, he heard that not far from the village was a Peach Cave in which He Xiangu dwelled.

He Xiangu is famous for her knowledge of herbs. Why not seek her guidance?

He decided to look for her.

After travelling for one whole day, he reached the foot of the mountain.

I've arrived.

He found the entrance to the cave.

Excuse me, are you He Xiangu?

As he did not dare to disturb the immortals, he decided to just stand aside and watch them play chess. Eventually, however, he could not resist calling out.

There are thousands of herbs all around and let me introduce them one by one.

She told him the names of the herbs and their properties.

Time passed quickly and the sky had turned dark.

Tienguai Li and I have an appointment. You stay here tonight and I'll send you back tomorrow.

The two immortals left by riding clouds.

One night passed.

The next day the herbalist found himself surrounded by precipices all around.

Have a meal first. I'll get a horse ready to send you back.

The herbalist found the meal extraordinarily tasty.

He Xiangu picked up some grass and started weaving.

164

She made a grass horse five inches long.

Then she made some incantations to it.

- - - - - - - - - -
- - - - - - - - - -

The grass horse turned into a live horse.

The herbalist found that his hoe and basket had rotted.

Spending a day here is equivalent to spending many years on earth.

Go!

Soon he saw the bridge in his village.

He landed safely on the bridge.

The horse neighed three times before flying back to the cave.

The herbalist found that the gate to his house had collapsed and only the perimeter wall remained.

The villagers could not recognize him.

Eventually, a white-haired old man recognized him.

The herbalist related his story to the villagers and they were stunned.

The herbalist later passed on his knowledge to future generations.

Since then the bridge on which the herbalist's horse landed became known as the Horse Landing Bridge.

The Eight Immortals Cross The Sea

In a certain year, the Eight Immortals were on their way home after attending the Peach of Immortality Gathering hosted by the Queen Mother on the third day of the third lunar month.

170

The Immortals were inebriated after attending the gathering.

Agreed!

Lü Dongbin hurled his sword across the sea.

The sword turned into a small boat which moved with the wind.

Tieguai Li turned his iron crutch into a piece of wood.

Han Xiangzi turned his flower basket into a boat. He Xiangu stood on a giant lotus.

Lan Caihe turned his jade board into a canoe while Cao Guojiu transformed his bamboo container into a raft.

Zhongli Quan stood on a huge banana leaf whereas Zhang Guolao rode on his paper donkey.

174

A ray of white light shone into the palace.

Sister, your chess technique is not bad.

What is this?
It is so blinding.

177

Wow! He Xiangu is so beautiful. Why not seize her to be my concubine?

The Immortals were enjoying themselves. Suddenly Han Xiangzi cried out. The others realized that He Xiangu was missing.

Xiangu!

They were no match for Lü Dongbin.

Lü Dongbin arrived at the Crown Prince's residence.

Dragon Crown Prince, release He Xiangu quickly!

What if I do not release her?

The Crown Prince and Lü Dongbin engaged in a fierce combat.

Lü Dongbin used his gourd to heat up the sea until it was boiling hot.

Dragon King's Palace

Lü Dongbin, how dare you charge into my palace. Do you know this is a heavenly offence?

Dragon King, do you know that your supposedly good son has taken He Xiangu by force?

183

186

188

The fierce battle shook heaven and earth.

191

Zhang Guolao's paper donkey cleared a path for the Immortals to leave the darkened palace.

A giant octopus had squirted a black liquid into the palace.

Let me deal with it.

Let's forget it. Otherwise when will such vengence end?

The Immortals decided to let the matter rest and return to the surface.

Eventually, the Immortals crossed the Eastern Sea in a happy mood.

196

Asiapac Comic Series (by Tsai Chih Chung)

Art of War
Translated by Leong Weng Kam
    The Art of War provides a compact set of principles essential for victory in battles; applicable to military strategists, in business and human relationships.

Book of Zen
Translated by Koh Kok Kiang
    Zen makes the art of spontaneous living the prime concern of the human being. Tsai depicts Zen with unfettered versatility; his illustrations spans a period of more than 2,000 years.

Da Xue
Translated by Mary Ng En Tzu
    The second book in the Four Books of the Confucian Classics. It sets forth the higher principles of moral science and advocates that the cultivation of the person be the first thing attended to in the process of the pacification of kingdoms.

Fantasies of the Six Dynasties
Translated by Jenny Lim
    Tsai Chih Chung has creatively illustrated and annotated 19 bizarre tales of human encounters with supernatural beings which were compiled during the Six Dyansties (AD 220-589).

Lun Yu
Translated by Mary Ng En Tzu
    A collection of the discourses of Confucius, his disciples and others on various topics. Several bits of choice sayings have been illustrated for readers in this book.

New Account of World Tales
Translated by Alan Chong
    These 120 selected anecdotes tell the stories of emperors, princes, high officials, generals, courtiers, urbane monks and lettered gentry of a turbulent time. They afford a stark and amoral insight into human behaviour in its full spectrum of virtues and frailties and glimpses of brilliant Chinese witticisms, too.

Origins of Zen
Translated by Koh Kok Kiang

Tsai in this book traces the origins and development of Zen in China with a light-hearted touch which is very much in keeping with the Zen spirit of absolute freedom and unbounded creativity.

Records of the Historian
Translated by Tang Nguok Kiong

Adapted from Records of the Historian, one of the greatest historical work China has produced, Tsai has illustrated the life and characteristics of the Four Lords of the Warring Strates.

Roots of Wisdom
Translated by Koh Kok Kiang

One of the gems of Chinese literature, whose advocacy of a steadfast nature and a life of simplicity, goodness, quiet joy and harmony with one's fellow beings and the world at large has great relevance in an age of rapid changes.

Sayings of Confucius
Translated by Goh Beng Choo

This book features the life of Confucius, selected sayings from The Analects and some of his more prominent pupils. It captures the warm relationship between the sage and his disciples, and offers food for thought for the modern readers.

Sayings of Han Fei Zi
Translated by Alan Chong

Tsai Chih Chung retold and interpreted the basic ideas of legalism, a classical political philosophy that advocates a draconian legal code, embodying a system of liberal reward and heavy penalty as the basis of government, in his unique style.

Sayings of Lao Zi
Translated by Koh Kok Kiang & Wong Lit Khiong

The thoughts of Lao Zi, the founder of Taoism, are presented here in a light-hearted manner. It features the selected sayings from Dao De Jing.

Sayings of Lao Zi Book 2
Translated by Koh Kok Kiang

In the second book, Tsai Chih Chung has tackled some of the more abstruse passages from the Dao De Jing which he has not included in the first volume of Sayings of Lao Zi.

Sayings of Lie Zi
Translated by Koh Kok Kiang

A famous Taoist sage whose sayings deals with universal themes such as the joy of living, reconciliation with death, the limitations of human knowledge, the role of chance events.

Sayings of Mencius
Translated by Mary Ng En Tzu

This book contains stories about the life of Mencius and various excerpts from "Mencius", one of the Four Books of the Confucian Classics, which contains the philosophy of Mencius.

Sayings of Zhuang Zi
Translated by Goh Beng Choo

Zhuang Zi's non-conformist and often humorous views of life have been creatively illustrated and simply presented by Tsai Chih Chung in this book.

Sayings of Zhuang Zi Book 2
Translated by Koh Kok Kiang

Zhuang Zi's book is valued for both its philosophical insights and as a work of great literary merit. Tsai's second book on Zhuang Zi shows maturity in his unique style.

Strange Tales of Liaozhai
Translated by Tang Nguok Kiong

In this book, Tsai Chih Chung has creatively illustrated 12 stories from the Strange Tales of Liaozhai, an outstanding Chinese classic written by Pu Songling in the early Qing Dynasty.

Zhong Yong
Translated by Mary Ng En Tzu

Zhong Yong, written by Zi Si, the grandson of Confucius, gives voice to the heart of the discipline of Confucius. Tsai has presented it in a most readable manner for the modern readers to explore with great delight.

Hilarious Chinese Classics by Tsai Chih Chung

Journey to the West 1

These books offer more than the all-too-familiar escapades of Tan Sanzang and his animal disciples. Under the creative pen of Tsai Chih Chung, *Journey to the West* still stays its course but takes a new route. En route from ancient China to India to acquire Buddhist scriptures, the Monk and his disciples veer off course frequently to dart into modern times to have fleeting exchanges with characters ranging from Ronald Reagan to Bunny Girls of the Playboy Club.

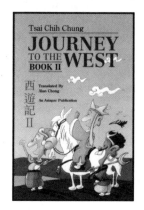

Journey to the West 2

Romance of the Three Kingdoms

Set in the turbulent Three Kingdoms Period, *Romance of the Three Kingdoms* relates the clever political manoeuvres and brilliant battle strategies used by the ambitious rulers as they fought one another for supremacy.

In this comic version, Tsai Chih Chung has illustrated in an entertaining way the four best-known episodes in the novel. Don't be surprised to see a warrior waving an Iraqi flag, a satellite dish fixed on top of an ancient Chinese building, and court officials playing mahjong or eating beef noodles, a favourite Taiwanese snack.

Strategy & Leadership Series by Wang Xuanming

Thirty-six Stratagems: Secret Art of War
Translated by Koh Kok Kiang (cartoons) &
Liu Yi (text of the stratagems)
A Chinese military classic which emphasizes deceptive schemes to achieve military objectives. It has attracted the attention of military authorities and general readers alike.

Six Strategies for War: The Practice of Effective Leadership
Translated by Alan Chong
A powerful book for rulers, administrators and leaders, it covers critical areas in management and warfare including: how to recruit talents and manage the state; how to beat the enemy and build an empire; how to lead wisely; and how to manoeuvre brilliantly.

Gems of Chinese Wisdom: Mastering the Art of Leadership
Translated by Leong Weng Kam
Wise up with this delightful collection of tales and anecdotes on the wisdom of great men and women in Chinese history, including Confucius, Meng Changjun and Gou Jian.

Three Strategies of Huang Shi Gong: The Art of Government
Translated by Alan Chong
Reputedly one of man's oldest monograph on military strategy, it unmasks the secrets behind brilliant military manoeuvres, clever deployment and control of subordinates, and effective government.

100 Strategies of War: Brilliant Tactics in Action
Translated by Yeo Ai Hoon
The book captures the essence of extensive military knowledge and practice, and explores the use of psychology in warfare, the importance of building diplomatic relations with the enemy's neighbours, the use of espionage and reconnaissance, etc.

Latest Titles in
Strategy & Leadership Series

Chinese Business Strategies

The Chinese are known for being shrewd businessmen able to thrive under the toughest market conditions. The secret of their success lies in 10 time-tested principles of Chinese entrepreneurship.

This book offers readers 30 real-life, ancient case studies with comments on their application in the context of modern business.

Sixteen Strategies of Zhuge Liang

Zhuge Liang, the legendary statesman and military commander during the Three Kingdoms Period, is the epitome of wisdom.

Well-grounded in military principles of Sun Zi and other masters before him, he excelled in applying them in state administration and his own innovations, thus winning many spectacular victories with his uncanny anticipation of enemy moves.

SPECIAL OFFER

Romance of the Three Kingdoms Vols. 1-10 in a NEW DISPLAY BOX!
China's Greatest Historical Classics in Comics

FREE: 216-page comics entitled "Sixteen Strategies of Zhuge Liang".
Free delivery.

Offer for Local Readers:

Original Price for 10 volumes	**S$99.91** (*inclusive of* GST)
*Special price for whole kit	**S$97.00** (*inclusive of* GST)

Send this complete page for your mail order

I wish to order _____ set(s) *of Romance of the Three Kingdoms **Vol. 1-10***

at the nett price of S$97.00 per kit.

Enclosed is my postal order/money order/cheque No. _____

for S$ _____

Name _____ **Tel** _____

Address _____

_____ Singapore _____

Send to: ASIAPAC BOOKS PTE LTD 629 Aljunied Road #04-06 Cititech Industrial Building
Singapore 389838 Tel: 7453868 Fax: 7453822

Note: Prices are subject to change without prior notice. ***Offer is for readers in Singapore only.***

SPECIAL OFFER

Strategy & Leadership Series

- [ ] Chinese Business Strategies
- [ ] Three Strategies of Huang Shi Gong
- [ ] Six Strategies for War
- [ ] Sixteen Strategies of Zhuge Liang
- [ ] Thirty-six Stratagems
- [ ] 100 Strategies of War
- [ ] Gems of Chinese Wisdom

Make your subscription for any 5 volumes or more of this comic series (tick box) and enjoy **20% discount**.
Original Price: S$15.90 per volume (*exclusive* of GST)
Offer at special discount (*inclusive of* postage):-

	5 Volumes	6 Volumes	7 Volumes
Singapore	68.30	82.20	95.30
Malaysia	71.60	88.30	101.00
International-by sea mail	78.60	100.30	113.00

* All Prices in Singapore Dollars. 3% GST charge for local orders.

I wish to subscribe for the above-mentioned titles

at the nett price of S$_____ (*inclusive of* postage)

- [ ] **For Singapore orders only:**
  Enclosed is my postal order/money order/cheque/ for S$ _____

  (No.: _____)

  For Singapore/Malaysia/International orders:

- [ ] Credit card. Please charge the amount of SIN$_____ to my credit card

VISA [ ]   Card No. _____ Card Holder's Name _____

MASTER [ ]   Expiry Date_____ Order Date_____ Signature _____

Name _____

Address _____

_____ **Tel** _____

Send to: ASIAPAC BOOKS PTE LTD 629 Aljunied Road #04-06 Cititech Industrial Building
          Singapore 389838 Tel: 65 -7453868 Fax: 65 -7453822
Note:
For this offer of 20% discount, there is no restriction on the titles ordered, that is, you may order any 5 or more of the series. Prices are subject to change without prior notice.